TEN CHAPTERS IN

THE LIFE

OF

JOHN HANCOCK.

NOW FIRST PUBLISHED SINCE 1789.

NEW YORK:

1857.

THE

WRITINGS

OF

LACO,

As published in the MASSACHUSETTS CENTINEL, in the months of February and March, 1789, with the addition of No. VII., which was omitted.

The Liberty of the Press is essential to the Security of Freedom in a State, it ought not, therefore, to be restrained in this Commonwealth.

MASSACHUSETTS BILL OF RIGHTS.

PRINTED AT BOSTON, 1789.

Printing Statement:

Due to the very old age and scarcity of this book, many of the pages may be hard to read due to the blurring of the original text, possible missing pages, missing text, dark backgrounds and other issues beyond our control.

Because this is such an important and rare work, we believe it is best to reproduce this book regardless of its original condition.

Thank you for your understanding.

WRITINGS OF LACO.

NO. I.

THE time for the election of Governour, &c., is near, and much has been, and will be said, to influence our votes in favour of the present Chief Magistrate. We are told, by his advocates, that he is the saviour of our country—that he has expended his estate and his health in its defence, and that we are indebted to him for all we have, and now enjoy, as a free people. And he himself has lately told the Legislature, that he is open and undisguised in his politicks. If it be true, that he has been a steady, uniform patriot, and has devoted his time, his health, and his estate to the publick service, he has certainly a strong claim to our gratitude, and may justly expect a general vote in his favour at the ensuing election—but if popular applause has been the alone object of his pursuit—if his health and estate has been devoted to this alone, and the publick good has had no influence upon his *political* conduct, we can be under no particular obligations to him, and are at full liberty to vote for the man that we may think best qualified to promote the publick felicity. To determine rightly upon this important question, we must enter carefully into his political character and conduct; and with candour consider his actions in publick life. In doing this, I care not to enter into a very minute detail of his doings as a publick man; but to touch only upon particular, important parts of his conduct. and to mark out the general leading principles of action with him: nor shall I think it proper, in the course of my narrative, to notice any attacks from hireling scribblers, or to attempt to answer any who do not *deny* the FACTS I may state, or contradict the OBSERVATIONS I may make as I go along.

Mr. H., by the death of his uncle, became possessed of a large estate. He was thought to have some of the exterior graces necessary to form a popular character, and he early discovered a strong inclination for popular applause. These qualities rendered him a proper object for the *effective patriots* of the day to bring forward to favour their views. They availed themselves of his great desire for popularity, and they represented him as a man useful in the cause of liberty, to give him importance in the eyes of the people—his vanity favoured their views—he was captivated with the idea of being a publick man—a man of the people—and he was lavish of his money, and in his attention to the people, to gain their affections. To render him conspicuous, they assigned him a part in their manœuvres, not important, but ostentatious; but having early discovered his caprice, they did not admit him to their private councils. Though they considered him as a useful instrument, and were desirous of retaining him in their service, they had no confidence in his attachment to their cause, nor did they ever intrust him with any thing that could much injure it, by being disclosed.

Upon these principles, and with these views, was he introduced into publick life, by the leaders of the opposition to Britain at that day. But though upon publick principles, he was introduced into the Legislature, and made to appear as a man of importance, he had not in fact any more efficiency, than the pen of the writer under the signature of MASSACHUSETTENSIS; and it was often with great pains they prevented him from going over to the other side. So great was his vanity, and so excessive his caprice, that his leaders were often at a loss to restrain and keep him steady. His character and his passions were so well known to *Bernard* and *Hutchinson*, &c., that they could always attempt his seduction with a prospect of success; and they would several times have gained him to their party, but for the vigilant eyes of the two Adamses, and Otis, &c. Nor did he, during the period I refer to, ever do a single honourable or important act that I have heard of, either by originating or carrying a measure, or furnishing money for any great and general purposes. Though lavish of his money, he always confined his gratuities to objects of the glaring, captivating kind, rather than to those really important, and extensively useful.

That such was Mr. H.'s political character and conduct, from his first introduction into publick life, to his being appointed a member of Congress, I verily believe; and I would refer those who may doubt it, to Mr. S. A., and others, who were his political creators and supporters, who knew every thing that took place at that time, and who have spoken freely and openly of his demerits. I would also refer them to the letters of *Hutchinson*, *Bernard*, and others, which have been published, for the proof of his wavering repeatedly, as to the side he should take; and for their ideas, as to his firmness or integrity. And yet, it was during this very period that he is said to have deserved so much of the publick, and to have conferred such obligations as can never be repaid. But I now call on his advocates to state the important transactions he there performed, or to show us how and in what instances he wasted his property to serve the publick, more than others did, of much less estate than he enjoyed.

The man who claims our suffrages, as a tribute

due to his services and patriotism, cannot take it
amiss that we inquire into the grounds of his claim.
It is fit and right that we do this in every instance,
or we must forfeit our title to the honourable distinc-
tion of free republicans, and shall by no means
honour him whom we favour with our votes. With
this sentiment impressed on my mind, I mean in
future numbers to pursue the inquiry into the claim
of Mr. H. to the supreme magistracy in this Commonwealth. I shall do it in a general way, except
in a few important, particular instances ; and shall
not, on the one hand, fear to animadvert freely nor
on the other, to lose sight of decency and candour,
Every man's conduct should be viewed with fair-
ness ; but tenderness seems peculiarly due to those,
whose lives are uncommonly marked with folly
and vice—since we must necessarily have a great
weight of prejudice upon our minds against them,
and shall naturally be inclined to view their actions
through a coloured medium.

NO. II.

In my last number, I gave a general view of
Mr. H.'s political character and conduct, from his
first entrance into publick life, to his going to Congress. A period important and critical—when the
feelings, the principles and the patriotism of men

were as much tried, as at any one, perhaps during our contest with Britain. But with all the advantages and endowments he then had to play the man, and to exert his talents in the publick service, I never heard of his doing any thing worthy of notice. or of his being considered by those, who knew his value, as any thing more than an instrument played on by others. Let us now see what part he acted as a member of Congress, and how far he contributed to effect our National Independence.

Mr. H. was happy in having for his colleagues men famous for their abilities, their virtues and their patriotism—men who were capable of extensive views and great actions; and who were resolved, for political purposes, to support him and make him conspicuous. They accordingly obtained his appointment to the chair of Congress. But, being elevated to the highest point through their agency, he thought them no longer necessary to his importance; and from the vanity and caprice, inherent in his nature, he attached himself to the tories, who were then in Congress. These men had perceived his love of flattery; they plied him closely and grossly; and they detached him from his colleagues, and led him to take a part in direct opposition to them, and to the feelings and interests of his constituents. In all questions for decisive measures against Britain, he hung back; and very much contributed to obstruct the Declaration of

Independence. The glare of Southern manners, and the parade of courtly living, engaged his affections; and he ever appeared to contemn the manly simplicity and firmness of the delegates from New England. Thus was a member from Massachusetts duped by the insidious tories—he was urged by them, who, by assiduous attention, led his vanity to give up the best interests of America, and to hazard even our independence itself, to increase his own popularity, or rather to gain new admirers.

When the important hour arrived that was to give birth to our country as a nation—when the pulse of his colleagues, as well as of a majority of Congress, and of the people at large, beat high for independence, and it was found the important question could no longer be put off, Mr. H. then gave a vote in favour of the measure, and put his official signature to that memorable Act of Congress, the Declaration of Independence.

With these facts in our mind, which are very notorious, and which Mr. S. A. and others can at any time verify, we naturally wonder, and smile at the extraordinary merit Mr. H. has assumed to himself, from the publication of that Declaration, with his name as president. The Secretary of Congress has as good a title to superior respect, for having certified the copy, as Mr. H. has for having signed the original—they were both mere official, mechanical acts, without any responsibility, such as the

most timid man upon the continent, in their situations, would not have hesitated to perform. Had
Mr. H. been a zealous promoter of the measure, he
would then have been entitled to an equal share of
veneration with those of his colleagues, who were
advocates for it ; but having been opposed to it
until it became inevitable, and reluctantly drawn in
with his vote in its favour, at the last moment, we
ought to resent his vanity and assurance in claiming
our first esteem and respect on that occasion.

If Mr. H. has been so active and efficient a man
as to merit the honourable appellation of "SAVIOUR
OF HIS COUNTRY," how is it that we can find no evidence of it in our published records, nor any traces
of such an idea upon the minds of any one of his
political cotemporaries ? Let his servile advocates
shew us upon the Journals of Congress the important
measures he originated—the special services he has
rendered—or the sums of money he has given to
relieve the exigencies of State. Or, if they do not
appear, then let them turn us to the page of our
own State records, or to our publick files, where we
may find the facts required. If we look into the
former we shall find many instances of the superior
wisdom and agency of the two Adamses, and many
other worthies ; and if we examine the latter, the
important labors of the same persons, as well as of a
Bowdoin, and others, will frequently appear, but
none of his. Why, then, is it, that he is thus arro-
gantly styled the "SAVIOUR OF HIS COUNTRY ?"

I never feel a disposition to detract from real merit; I rather err in giving way to grateful or respectful feelings too much; but, when a tribute is demanded, with all the pride of vanity and insolence, which I know is not due, I feel for my own and my country's honour, and spurn at the injustice of the claim. From his first entrance into public life to his return from Congress, I never could learn of any extraordinary merit or services of his; on the contrary, he certainly is indebted to an uncommon concurrence of circumstances, which led his colleagues to give him importance for publick purposes. Never was there a man more eminently the child of fortune than Mr. H.—he has shared largely in the reputation and laurels acquired by others, and has enjoyed a princely fortune without any labour or exertions of his own. Possessing the exterior graces in an eminent degree, and inheriting qualities adapted to please in polite circles, he might have passed through the private walks of life with real eclat; but fired with ambition, and devoted to popularity, he has assumed characters, and taken situations, which he could not support with credit to himself, or advantage to the publick. But he has become so vain of the reputation he has fortuitously enjoyed, and has been so flattered and pampered by his dependants, tha he cannot brook any thing like independence in others, and always frowns on that man that has any opinion or will of his own.

14

And hence it is that we find him so averse to
associate with men of real respectability. His
habits and disposition, though they may for a time
make him a popular man, or give him importance
in the eyes of the populace, are widely different
from those great and useful qualities, which ought
to adorn the character of our chief magistrate; and,
unless we are quite ignorant of men and things,
they will certainly be viewed as real disqualifications
for that important office—nor can we ever elect
such a man to rule over us without doing violence
to our reason, our conscience, and our social interests. If, therefore, we do not find in his political
conduct, subsequent to his return from Congress,
habits and principles opposite to those which have
before governed his actions, we cannot deliberately
make him the man of our choice; nor shall we feel
ourselves justified in styling him the "SAVIOUR OF
OUR COUNTRY." Whether such a change is to be
found in his sentiments and conduct after that period, shall be the inquiry of a future number.

----◆----

NO. III.

THAT there is a tide in the affairs of men every
attentive observer must be convinced of; but among
all the tides that may affect them, there is none so
irregular and uncertain in its motions as that of

popular applause and affection. So eccentric and
precarious is its course and continuance that few
men of character are willing to trust themselves
afloat upon it, lest they should make shipwreck of
a good reputation; but the popular demagogues,
who have every thing to hope, and nothing to fear,
these are always ready to take their chance in the
current, and they frequently change, by it, their
situations for the better. Feathers and chaff, we
know, are safely wafted about on the surface, and
take any direction which the tide may happen to
give them; but an object of weight and magnitude
will often be caught up by the shallows, or be cast
ashore by the eddies and whirlpools. This figure has
often accounted to me for the continued popularity
of such men as Mr. H., and we have frequently seen
that the pliant twig will, by bending, retain its situation, when, by the force of the torrent, the sturdy oak
will be torn up by the roots. No man, however,
will be so foolish as to say that the former is so
reputable in our view as the latter, or that we may
rest in safety our weight against the one as well as
against the other.

But perhaps it will be said, that if we have not
hitherto discovered Mr. H.'s superior merit in the
political line, we must allow him to have made a
great figure as a military man; and the expedition
to Rhode Island will be mentioned as the instance
in which he exhibited his warlike talents, and ren-

dered his country the most important services. On this field I should wish to draw a veil, and conceal it from the world, from a strong native disposition I have, to cover defects and weaknesses incident to our nature, but, as much has been required of us for his great services and exertions on that occasion, we ought to inquire how far the demand is well founded, and how great the obligation conferred.

Mr. H. was Major General of the Militia, at the time that memorable expedition was set on foot. He ever had a great fondness for parade of every *kind*, insomuch that he always eagerly sought after even that of the most puerile kind; and upon this principle it is, that he was never known to decline any appointment, from a Clerk of the Market to a President of Congress. Having heard much of the pleasures of the camp, and conceiving this a fine opportunity to pluck a military laurel without any danger to his person, he sought, and obtained the command of our militia.—He appointed his aids— he prepared his accoutrements—and, with all the parade of a veteran conqueror, he issued his orders, and made the necessary arrangements to march to the field.—When he got to Rhode Island, he took an eligible situation for his quarters—he appeared on the parade *en militaire*—he sallied out often for the sake of air and exercise, and he sometimes approached so near to the enemy, under the idea of reconnoitring, as to distinguish, by the aid of a good perspective, that the British flag was still flying at some miles' distance. Martial musick and military movements alone delighted ; and never was the fire of military ambition so conspicuous in any man's countenance and conduct, excepting the instance of the R——y hero, when he summoned the garrison of Fort Independence to surrender. But this flame was of short duration.—The severe cannonade at the arrival of the French fleet, though at several miles' distance, disordered his nerves ; the sound of the drum disturbed his muscles, by alarming his fears ; and his nightly slumbers were short and uncertain, from the lively scenes of blood and carnage, which a heated imagination was continually presenting to his view.

This situation was too painful and humiliating for the *Man of the People* long to endure. He grew peevish and uneasy—he complained of the length and tediousness of the campaign—and he talked frequently of quitting the field. This, his aids, who were men of spirit, were fearful would soon happen. They felt for his, and their own honour ; they used every argument to allay his fears—to compose his nerves—and to awake his ambition, and were in hopes to succeed. But the departure of the fleet, the roar of the cannon as they passed the lines of the enemy, and the smell of the powder, which by a southerly wind was unfortunately conveyed to his nose ; the combined influence of these horrid circumstances, was too much for our hero to support. He resolved to return home—he dreamed that his child was sick and dying—he fancied that the fleet had gone to Boston, and could not refit in his absence; but more than this, he imagined that the British were roused, and he could not believe it safe or prudent, for the man of the people to remain any longer on the Island.—His last idea proved at once decisive, and off he set with a quick step. In vain were the remonstrances of his aids and others—in vain was the suggestion of the evil effects upon the army—and in vain all intimations of injury to his own honour. His fears were more powerful than all other passions together; and he flattered himself, that by urging his great anxiety for the safety of the fleet, as the cause of his flight, he might save his reputation. To favour this pretence, he flew through the country with astonishing speed—he inquired of the farmer at work in his barn, whether he had seen or heard any thing of the fleet. So swift was his flight, and so strange his inquiries, that the people on the road conceived him to have been an express, who had disordered his brain by the rapidity of his motion. Having good cattle, he reached home in a few hours, and the first question upon entering the town, was, as to the safety of the fleet; but after being at rest a little time, and finding himself safe in his own house, his fears subsided—his solicitude for the fleet abat-

ed—and he enjoyed his pleasures as well as ever—
he recounted his exploits in the field, and gave a
lively description of the enemy's alarm when he
reconnoitered their posts.

Thus ended Mr. H.'s memorable campaign to
Rhode Island; and these were the laurels he gather-
ed in that famous expedition. If it be thought that
they are not of the best tint possible, it should be
remembered that he cropt them flying, and had not
time to select the best plants.

But to treat this important subject with more
seriousness, I would ask, who that had the feelings
of a man, or more than that, the feelings of a patriot, which he pretended to have, would have left
the camp at so critical a moment; when the British
were expected to attack the American army, and
every one was anxious for the safety of our country
and its cause. Mr. H. commanded a large body of
militia for this State, which formed no small part of
our army. Among them were a considerable number of respectable gentlemen as volunteers. These,
as well as Mr. H. had conceived an idea, that, with
the assistance of the French, the capture of the
British army on Rhode Island was the work of a
day; they had only to shew themselves and the
business was done.—They viewed the expedition
rather as a party of pleasure, than the serious campaign, which would terminate in the fighting of
armies. But when the French fleet went away,
and the British were expected to become the assail-

ants, the matter wore a serious aspect; and the fate of our country was thought, in a good degree, to depend upon the success of that expedition. Under such circumstances, Mr. H. was called upon by every principle, both publick and private, to play the MAN, and await the issue. A regard to his own honour, and the safety of his country, should have raised him above all concern for his personal safety, or the enjoyment of his friends and family at home. If he who was comfortably guarded against the weather by good quarters—who was entirely exempted from all the fatigues of personal duty, and who could not probably be called into the way of personal danger, could not muster resolution to remain for a few days; what could he expect from the gentlemen volunteers, who did the duty of private soldiers, and in case of action, must have encountered the toil and dangers of their station. He ought, as their commander, to have set them an example worthy of their imitation; and to have encouraged them to duty, by sharing cheerfully in their toils and dangers. But instead of this, the General was amongst the first, if not the very first, to leave the Island, in a time of danger; he deserted the post he sought after, and most unworthily filled; and he left the gentlemen who accompanied him, and the troops he commanded to shift for themselves, or fall a prey to the British. Instead of persuading his officers and men, by his own example,

willingly to submit to soldiers' fare, and to keep
those quiet under the hardships of their station, who
had before been accustomed to elegance and luxury;
he was always studying new means of dissipation,
and kept carriages constantly passing to supply him
with delicacies from hence.

It is well worthy of observation, that Mr. H.
after his return from Rhode Island had a grant of
40,000 dollars, I think it was, while the gentlemen volunteers, who attended him, and who were
at as much necessary expense as he was perhaps,
having raised companies of volunteers for that expedition, received nothing from Government. Whether that grant was made him to defray the expences
of a luxurious table, which had a direct tendency
to create an uneasiness among the gentlemen volunteers who accompanied him, and which was very
improper in any point of view ; or whether it was
for the extraordinary speed with which he fled from
the appearance of danger notwithstanding the pressing intreaties of General GLOVER, who stated to
him the evil tendency of such an example, and very
justly foretold the effect it would have among the volunteers and militia, and upon his own reputation,
those only can tell who solicited it for him. But this
is certainly true, that he was at no extraordinary
expence, but such as was highly disreputable and
injurious to the service, nor did his presence answer
any other purpose, than to create uneasiness among

the volunteers and militia, and to bring dishonour on him for his precipitate flight at the only moment when he, and those who followed him, could have been of any service. This however is imprudently stated by his puffers, as one of those instances, in which he has wasted his own property in the service of the publick.

I would now ask, where was the merit of this unsoldier-like conduct? How or at what time, did he serve the publick by this expedition, or do honour to himself? Did he not on the contrary do as much injury to the country, and dishonour to himself as he could do by an evil example? Was there any thing in his conduct upon this occasion, that was not opposite to that of a Hero, or the "Saviour of his Country?" Did he not leave those, who followed him from personal attachment to the field, in a very dangerous situation, and in a most disgraceful manner; and was the eventual escape of the troops, which he led, from the hands of the British, in any degree owing to his attention, firmness or prudence?

———◆———

NO. IV.

Honour and reputation in publick life, can be acquired only by a right discharge of the duties of the stations we occupy; and not merely by the rank or the importance of the office, to which we may by accident have been elevated. Time and change frequently raise men to posts, of which they are wholly unworthy; and, in popular governments more especially, we often see men elevated to places, for which they have no qualifications, and as it would seem at first view, purposely to render them conspicuously ridiculous. This consideration ought to make us cautious and diffident, how far we avail ourselves of the popular tide in our favour; but, unfortunately both for Mr. H. and the publick, it has had no weight upon his mind. He has eagerly received every thing that was offered him by the people, without any such reflections; and has frequently accepted of appointments, to which he was not only unequal, but which were wholly incompatible with those he had before enjoyed. Let him be hailed master, and receive homage from the multitude, and he cares not what is the real opinion of the respectable part of society, as to him or his conduct. This has been clearly verified, in that part of his publick life we have before examined. We will now attend to subsequent periods.

When our new Constitution was forming in 1780, Mr. H. was a delegate from Boston, in Convention; and never surely was there a more happy opportunity for a man to display his knowledge of the principles of government, and of men and things. Numbers of members did honour to them-

selves and their country, on that occasion; and
our present happy Constitution, the wonder of the
world, exhibits the clearest proof of wisdom and
knowledge. But has Mr. H. a fair claim to a large
share of the fame due to its compilers? Which of
its principal beauties and excellencies did he pro-
ject? Or which of its most valuable checks originated with him? Let the active men upon that
stage declare, and do him justice; or let them say,
whether he had any more merit upon that great
occasion, than those had, who gave a mere silent
vote in its favour—I never could learn that he had.

The Constitution being adopted, Mr. H. was the
man first elected to the chair of government;
and never did a man take the reins in his hands,
with so many fortunate circumstances in his favour.
Pleased as we all were with the constitution itself,
and enjoying, as he then did, the affections of a
great part of the people, he might by a wise and
prudent administration, have secured a lasting reputation to himself, and derived to the publick all
the benefits, which were so sanguinely expected
from the new constitution. But we soon saw, that he
was incapable of a wise and prudent administration,
as he had before proved himself of framing a form
of government. No sooner was he in office, than he
began to indulge his ruling passions. He, it is said,
made nominations to offices the most important,
without any regard to the qualifications of the per-

sons, or the good of society; and that the only
inquiries he in general made, were, whether the
persons who applied, or were proposed as candi-
dates for an office, were his friends, and had given
him their votes. These being the principles upon
which he made nominations, many valuable men
were prevented from being made useful to the
community; and hence proceeded a swarm of jus-
tices, sheriffs, &c., who have by their ignorance
and folly, injured the reputation of government,
perverted the laws, and proved a curse to society,
for it happened, unfortunately for the publick in
that respect, that those who voted against him,
were generally men of the most repute for their
wisdom and virtue. He availed himself of the
prerogative of his office, to hedge himself about,
and strengthen his interest, by giving places to his
advocates. And he has always refused, except in
a few instances, where the voice of the people became irresistible, to nominate any who were not
his personal friends.

The evils resulting to the state from this unjust,
or, at best, wanton exercise of his prerogative, have
been much greater and more extensive than is generally imagined. The bulk of the people know but
little of the government under which they live.
They hear but little of the conduct of those at the
head of affairs; and they see less. Their opinions
of government are formed, principally at least,

from the character and conduct of magistrates and other executive officers, who live near them. When therefore they perceive, that those offices are filled by men of contemptible, or worse characters, they naturally conclude, that as the stream is foul, the fountain cannot be pure; and feeling also as they always must in such cases, that the laws become grievances, by being weakly and wickedly executed, they soon get to despise the government itself, and grow ripe for a revolution. These, I conceive, are the natural effects of such improper appointments to office; and the insurrections in 1785 were clearly a living proof of it. Government had then lost all its dignity, from the causes I have mentioned, in the eyes of the multitude; and the evils of that day were the natural fruit of the seeds sown by Mr. H. when first in the chair.

It is the part of a patriot, and especially of one placed at the head of a free republick by the suffrages of the people, to teach them both by precept and example, to practice those virtues proper to their situation, and necessary to their safety and happiness—such as temperance, frugality, prudence, and a love of their country; and the more critical the affairs of the publick, and pressing its wants, the more necessary is the general practice of those social virtues, and the greater the obligations on the leaders of the people to set them a good example. But how opposite to this was the conduct of Mr. H.

through the whole course of his first administration. We were then in the midst of our contest with Britain; and great were the exigencies of the State; both for men and money. The calls upon the people to support the war, were frequent and pressing; and our affairs required from them every thing that was not necessary to their own subsistence. In this situation, industry and economy seemed to be essential to our safety and happiness; and our case then demanded from men high in office, and especially of those who had assumed the character, and expected the veneration due to eminent patriots, the full weight of precept and example. But instead of this, Mr. H. has exhibited to our view continued scenes of luxury, to the great distress of the *venerable old* PATRIOT, as he is eminently styled, and as an evil example to the people, who are prone to imitate those, whom they consider as their betters. At one period, and that a distressed one too, nothing was heard of from Mr. H., but balls, routs, and all the various fascinating pleasures of European courts. They followed each other in such constant, rapid succession, for several months, and the citizens of all ages, ranks and descriptions, were so generally made to partake of them, that it seemed as if he meant to have drowned their fears and distresses by music, dancing and feasting. He at length carried these scenes of dissipation so far, that the sober citizens, who had shared in his pleasures, were very uneasy for their own credit. This was so apparent, that it soon prevented the usual attention at his parties; his guests by degrees withdrew from his board; and by their conduct, became silent reprovers, at least, of such dangerous and evil examples. These are truths too notorious to be denied. If such conduct has had any share in delivering us from the yoke of Britain—if it had any thing in it that looked like patriotism, or had any tendency to save us from political destruction, let him be so far viewed as a patriot, and the saviour of his country; but no further.

NO. V.

It is an unpleasant task to display to the world the foibles and defects of a weak fellow-mortal; and to deprive him of a reputation which he never deserved, or to strip him of virtues which he never possessed but from the courtesy of his friends, may appear to be envious. Charity and benevolence are pleasing virtues—they engage our esteem and affection: and happy would it be for society if they had a more general influence upon our lives and conduct. But we often entertain false ideas of those amiable qualities, as well as of modesty, courage, &c., and, from a superficial view of things, we often approve of that which is directly opposed to them.

True benevolence to man most certainly consists in promoting the greatest possible happiness of society; but it sometimes so happens that this cannot be effected without inducing a partial evil. To rob a butterfly of its gaudy plumage, appears, in the abstract, to be a malevolent action; but if, by doing it, one could save the life of a man, or promote the happiness of thousands, it would be deemed meritorious. Thus, though I may, by my inquiries, give pain to Mr. II., yet, as he has had a strong and a baneful influence upon our social happiness, from the weight of affairs, and his improper exercise of its duties—as from wrong ideas of his true character as a publick man, we have ourselves contributed to increase the evil, by continuing him in office, it must be right to undeceive the publick, or to provide an antidote against the poisonous charms of his popular influence, I should cheerfully embrace a fair opening to give him some praise, as a publick man; but, I seriously declare, I have not discovered one. Was I to follow him into private life, I should there find a more variegated scene, and might collect many handsome things to be said in his favour; but I mean not to notice either his failings or virtues in private life.

Being at the head of our government during the most trying scenes of our contest with Britain, he had a full knowledge of our wants and dangers; for all communications from Congress and the army were addressed to him. With this evidence always before him, would not the patriot's breast have been filled with anxiety, and prompted to exertion? Would not his mind have been continually upon the stretch to devise ways and means to relieve the exigencies of State? But, instead of this, Mr. H. was at this very period in the height of his dissipated course. The hours which should have been devoted for projecting those means, and preparing the business necessary for the legislature to take up, was wholly engrossed by his pleasures; and, during the course of four years' war, I never could learn that he suggested one idea to the court for alleviating burthens upon the people; nor did I ever hear that he sacrificed either his time, his pleasures, or his property to serve the publick. When the inability of Government to provide for an immediate demand of men or money was apparent, the aid of individuals by way of subscription became often necessary. Upon such, and other occasions, he frequently lent his name, but he very seldom furnished the money he subscribed; and, so far has he been from sacrificing his property to publick purposes, that I verily believe he has done it less than any other man of equal ability in the State. That it is the peculiar appropriate duty of the Governor, as head of the Executive, to receive and examine all publick dispatches, is evident from the uniform practice of their being addressed to

him; and that it is also his duty to manage the
publick business, in the recess of the court, no one
will deny. By a clear and judicious statement of
that kind, with the proper documents laid before
them, the sessions of the General Court, during the
five years Mr. H. was first in the chair, need not
have been half so long as they were, and the publick business have been much better done. We may
say, upon a fair calculation, that by a proper attention to that part of the duties of his station, he
might have saved to the State more than 10,000
dollars a year in the pay of the court only; and
have prevented most of those acts and resolves
which, from their interference with pre-existing laws,
or being wrong in principle or form, from the hasty
manner in which they were passed, it became necessary soon to repeal. Where, then, was that
engaging trait in his character which has of late
been so conspicuous and celebrated? Was his
economy then feeble and in its infancy? Or was it
lulled asleep by the fascinating charms of balls and
routs? Or would he not steal one hour in the day
from those favourite amusements for such important
purposes? This seems to be a small portion of
time, but it would have been enough for the purpose, perhaps; and is, beyond a doubt, much more
than he used then to devote to such business:—I
cannot, indeed, find any evidence of his having
applied to it at all. If we look over the files and

records of that day, we shall find hundreds of the most important letters from Congress, from General Washington, and our members of Congress, that were never answered, though the subject of them required the most speedy answers; nor does it appear that he took any order whatever respecting. or had ever read them. His custom was, when the court had convened, to send them down a chaos of papers and leave them to make the best use of them they could.

But the injury to the State from this shameful neglect of duty in Mr. H., both to its interest and reputation, appears much greater in another view of the matter. Had he kept up a correspondence with our members of Congress and the Executives of our sister States, we should not only have known more of what was passing in Congress, and in the other States, but our Delegates would have been better informed of the views, interests and doings of the General Court, and their constituents at large. It is a degrading truth, that our own Government knew as much of the doings of the British Parliament. as of Congress, and much more, than they did of the other States; and our members knew very much more of the politicks of the other States, than they did of this. The reason was, that every post brought regular advices to the other members from their respective Governours, which were frequently communicated to our members; but our members

of Congress were frequently, for six months together, without any official communication from their
own Government. This was so very injurious and
disgraceful to the State, that the *venerable old* PA-
TRIOT procured the appointment of a committee
of the General Court, in 1781, I think it was, to keep
up the necessary intercourse with the other States,
Congress, and our own members. If we had received and given the proper information, as the
other States did, we might, with them, have avoided
a great part of our present State debt. When any
officers called for aid from the States of Pennsylvania,
York, or Jersey, &c., the supplies were furnished,
and the persons who did it, either looked to the
Congress in the first instance, for his pay ; or if the
State made payment, they soon obtained through
the Delegates, a resolve allowing them to deduct it
from an existing requisition. By those means they
avoided incurring a large debt for supplies on Continental account, as we did in this State; and are
now free from the embarrassments which we feel so
heavily. Had Mr. H. done as others in the same
station in our sister States, we might have had the
same information, and have made the same prudent
use of it as they did; but our General Court knew
nothing of such modes of getting relief, nor did our
members in Congress know, that we were here
making such advances on Continental account.
Both were kept in ignorance of what was passing,

through his neglect; whereas they ought both to have had a regular and full information of all that passed on their respective theatres, through his official agency, and being fully apprised of all that materially affected the interest of the State. The amount of the saving which might have been in this way made, it is not easily precisely to say; but the best judges are of opinion, that we might, at least, have avoided one-third part of our present debt. And what renders him the more inexcusable is, that he was often informed of the load of debt, which the State was then assuming, and of the means which the other States were then using, to avoid it with respect to themselves.

If in this part of his administration he made sacrifices of any kind, to his private injury or inconvenience, to serve the publick, let him have the credit of it; but from the above statement, which many must recollect to be true, and which our files and records will verify, I think it is clear, that he sacrificed both the interest and the reputation of the State to his own pleasure and caprice.

NO. VI.

It is a republican maxim, that publick men are but the servants of the people; and it is always expected, that those who engage in the service of the

State, are bound not only to a conscientious discharge of the duties of office, but in every possible
way to promote the happiness of the community.
This principle is rational and just—it ought to have
an habitual influence on the conduct of those who
engage in the service of the people ; and to defeat
their just expectations, by a wilful neglect of duty,
should always entail upon the delinquent, the most
pointed disgrace, and severe reprehension. But it
sometimes happens, from a concurrence of causes,
that the greatest delinquencies of this sort, are for
a long time, concealed from the eyes of the people,
and we are led, upon publick principles, to view those
as our chief benefactors, who have really proved,
by their weakness and indiscretion, highly injurious
to the State. This has been precisely the case with
Mr. H. For good reasons, no doubt, he has been
passed upon as for much more than his real value,
for a number of years: and we have been in the
habit of considering him as our greatest patriot,
and one, who has more wisdom and efficiency than
any among us. This idea we have taken implicitly
from others, and from our having seen him so often
and so high in office; but upon inquiry we find,
that he was placed in those stations from very different motives by others, and, that the same persons
have prevented us from seeing more than one side
of his portrait. But as the principles which rendered that deception not only justifiable but merito-

rious, no longer can operate, we ought now to have
the veil taken from our eyes, and be permitted to
take a fair view of his political character and conduct; and to judge for ourselves, as to the obligations we are under to Mr. H. for his publick services.
This has been the alone object of my past inquiry;
and will direct me in the future. I do assure you,
that I have frequently had, in the course of these
papers, true benevolent Shandean ideas enter my
mind; and have been upon the point of exclaiming,
"Away with thee; why should I hurt thee," &c.
But reason came in, and took off the force of one's
feelings by suggesting, that it was high time we
should distinguish characters.

Our Chief Magistrate represents the dignity and
sovereignty of the State; he has a yearly salary of
near 4,000 dollars, to enable him to entertain respectable strangers who come here, and who pay him in his
official capacity a proper respect; and to live in a
style proper to his station. This is by no means an
unimportant part of his duty—for strangers naturally form their opinion of the Government and State,
from what they may observe in the principal officers. Upon this principle, how many times have
we been distressed for the reputation of the State,
when we have seen Mr. H. actuated by a levity and
caprice that would dishonour a very young man sud-
denly elevated. It is needless here to repeat instances—they must be fresh in the memory of every

one in the least acquainted with his conduct—and will long be remembered by foreigners.

These various indecencies, and impropriety of conduct, and the manifest neglect of the duties of his office, evidently lessened him in the eyes of the people. To check this growing disaffection, and to stimulate his friends to more exertion in his favour, he resolved, in 1785, to make a show of resigning his office. This artifice had before several times answered his purpose; and he now expected, that his friends in the legislature would have obtained a vote, that his continuance in the chair was essential to the safety and happiness of the State. This was what he wanted to revive his popularity; and he then would have made a merit of continuing in office, to oblige the people, and promote their happiness. Relying on such being the effect, he sent to the Legislature a formal resignation; and plead an inability to perform the duties of his office, from an ill state of health, as the motive of his conduct. But he was deceived in his idea of the temper of the Court.—They wished to get rid of him, and gladly accepted of his resignation. Thus caught in his own trap he grew sour and malevolent in his temper. He did all he could to irritate, and create an opposition in the people at large, to the succeeding administration. This we may conclude from his own insidious suggestions, and the manifest language and conduct of his dependents.—They re-

presented his successor in office as an arbitrary man;
and they asserted that all taxes upon the people
were imposed without necessity and purposely intended to impoverish and subjugate them. By a
constant and assiduous circulation of such false-
hoods, and the inflammatory writings of the "*un-
principled Honestus*," they at length excited an
uneasiness among the ignorant and unwary.

No sooner did they discover that a fire was en-
kindled, than they most industriously exerted themselves to blow it into a flame. A quondam and unworthy member of an honourable bench, and a certain chattering changeling, who aspired, without
merit, at political elevation—these laboured more
abundantly to increase the disaffection, and for the
avowed purpose of getting Mr. H. again into the
chair; and no doubt, with his privity and concurrence, for they were nightly plodding with him to
promote their design. The official and professional
opinions of the former of these men, led the ignorant people to believe, that the courts of law were
a nuisance—the senate a grievance—taxes unlawful
and oppressive—government cruel—and the governour a tyrant. The same sentiments were echoed
by the latter of them with all the zeal and declama-
tion of a fanatic preacher, at the corners of the
streets, and in the most publick places. He also
added, that the Constitution itself was greatly de-
fective—that the people were all equal, and on

a level, having the same rights to plac⸳s and property—that if Mr. H. was again in the chair, halcyon days would at once commence—no more taxes be required, and like Sergeant Kite, he laboured to persuade the people, that they might then " buy a goose for a groat, and sell the feathers for a shilling." So zealous was the Changeling in exciting insurrections, that, when engaged in a harangue, he would not even shorten it, though he were told, that his patients were dying by the dozen.

By these means, for these purposes, and through their agency, was an alarming and open insurrection actually produced. This was the point which Mr. H. and his advocates, above referred to, had been anxiously wishing for ; and their object was now to make the most of it. But the matter had now become serious—the citizens of Boston became deeply interested ; and they warmly supported the measures of government. This apparently damped the ardour of Mr. H. and his "immaculate" friends. They became more cautious, but not less active in encouraging the insurgents. They kept up a constant intercourse, it was said, and they all openly condemned the conduct of government. It was industriously circulated all over the State, that Mr. H. had said, that he could reduce the insurgents to duty only by talking to them—that Mr. Quondam had said, as a professional man, that government had no authority from the Constitution to use force with them—and that Mr. Changeling had said, that the insurrection was nothing more than a harmless ebullition of the true republican principle—he also had said, that the sight of Mr. H.'s baises, like relicks of eminent saints, would work miracles; it would restore order among the insurgents, and lead them at once to beat their swords into plough-shares.

If in this part of his political course we have discovered evident marks of the great statesman and patriot — if he has made his own interest, views and interest quite subservient to the publick good, let us sound his praises, and hail him as the Saviour of our Country. But if, on the contrary, we perceive, that a selfish ambition, and a puerile levity, have uniformly guided his conduct and opinions, we ought to lament our past veneration for an unworthy character, and resolve for the future to be more vigilant and wary.

—————

NO. VII.

THERE are men in every free society, who have not a common interest with the community at large. and who rely wholly on the popular affection in their favour to give them promotion and support in publick life. They are too proud and restless in their tempers, and too indolent in their habits, and

capricious in their pursuits, to provide for themselves by any common avocations; and, having no
other objects to attend to, they are generally too
successful in their endeavours to excite the passions,
and engage the voice of the people on their side.
Without abilities to make them really useful in publick life, and devoid of principles or merits that can
command respect, they have no dependence but
upon popular inattention to bring them into view;
and, having been long attentive to the popular pulse,
and always acquainted with the darling object with
the multitude for the time, they rarely fail to touch
the right string, and to make the people subserve
their own selfish and private views. Upon these
principles we may fairly account for the conduct
and success of the seekers and demagogues of our
times. We have often seen the public mind highly
agitated by their artifices; but have generally been
too careless and superficial in our inquiries, to trace
the evil to its source, and, of course, have been
mistaken in the remedies we have applied. There
cannot be found within the compass of our memory an instance so strongly verifying the prece-
ding observation, as that of Mr. H. and his adher-
ing dependents. It was a time of commotion that
first gave him political existence; and it was to render those commotions beneficial to our country,
that induced our patriots of that day, to think of
giving him importance. Many of us can remember

the pains they took, and the address they made use of, to keep up the idea; and while it was important to the publick that the impression should remain, they were so fortunate as to preserve it. But in a short time after the peace in 1783, when our passions had subsided, and our sober reason took the lead — when we had leisure and inclination to think for ourselves, and no one thought it necessary, upon publick principles, any longer to keep a veil over Mr. H. and his conduct, we soon began to discover his foibles and weakness, and he rapidly sunk in our esteem. This gave rise, as we have seen in our last number, to his capricious resignation; and that, in its effects, to the late insurrections.

The alarming situation of our affairs at that period, and the part which Mr. H. and his adherents acted, both before and after he was again seated in the chair, is too recent and fresh in our minds to require a detail of facts. Suffice it to say, that it was exactly after the old manner; and wholly adapted to promote his own personal, popular views, without any regard to the dignity or safety of the government. And the course of his conduct from his reassuming the chair, to the meeting of our State Convention, for considering and adopting the new form of government for the Union, was nothing more than a renewed exhibition of the same levities, and a uniform preference of his own private interest to that of the publick.

A scene now opens upon us, very interesting
and important:—The objects which then presented
for our consideration, were so novel, and of such
magnitude, as deservedly engrossed the feelings and
the attention of every man. No one could remain
mute and indifferent, while the question as to the new
Constitution was pending; and every one, who felt
no other bias than a regard to the safety and happiness of our country must necessarily create, was most
anxiously solicitous for its adoption. But the popular
demagogues, and those were very much embarrassed
in their affairs, united to oppose it with all their might;
and they laboured incessantly, night and day, to
alarm the simple and credulous, by insinuating, that,
however specious its appearance, and that of its advocates, tyranny and vassalage would result from its
principles. The former of those descriptions were
conscious, that a stable and efficient government,
would deprive them of all their future importance,
or support from the publick; and the latter of them
knew, that nothing but weakness and convulsions
in government could screen them from payment of
their debts. How far Mr. H. was influenced by
either, or both of these motives, it is not easy to
determine; but no one, who recollects his general
habits, who knows his situation and views, and was
acquainted with the open conversation and conduct
of his cabinet counsellors, can have a doubt of his
being opposed to it. We all know, that Mr. Quon-

dam and Mr. Changeling, as well as the once venerable old patriot, who by a notable detection has .
thrown himself into the arms of Mr. H. in violation
of every principle; and for the paltry privilege of
sharing in his smiles, has, at the eve of life, cast an
indelible stain over his former reputation—it is well
known, I say, that these men do not dare to speak
in publick, a language opposite to that of their
patron; and it is equally notorious, that they were
open in their opposition to the Constitution. They
even went so far as to vilify its compilers, that they
might thence draw an argument to support their
suggestions, of its containing the seeds of latent
tyranny and oppression. They endeavoured by
every possible means in their power, to create a
popular clamour against the Constitution; but they
failed in their attempt; and Mr. H. and his friends
were obliged, upon their own principles, to grow
more cautious in their opposition. The good sense
of the *Mechanicks* of Boston, had produced some
manly and spirited resolutions, which effectually
checked Mr. H. and his followers in their opposition to the Constitution; and eventually occasioned
four votes in its favour, which otherwise would have
been most certainly against it. Had those resolutions not made their appearance, Mr. H. and three
others of our delegates would have been in the
negative; but it was thought necessary by them,
after they had appeared, to vote in favour of it.

Having settled this point, the next thing was to do
it with a good grace, and to profit as much by it as
they could; and Mr. H. accordingly intimated to
the advocates for the adoption, that he would appear
in its favour, if they would make it worth his while.
This intimation was given through a common friend
who assured the friends of the Constitution, that
nothing more would be required on the part of Mr.
H. than a promise to support him in the chair at the
next election. This promise, though a bitter pill, was
agreed to be given; for such was the state of things,
that they were very much afraid to decide upon the
question, whilst he was opposed to it. The famous
conciliatory proposition of Mr. H. as it was called,
was then prepared by the advocates, and adopted
by him, but the truth is he never was consulted
about it, nor knew its contents, before it was handed
to him to bring forward in Convention. At the
appointed time Mr. H. with all the parade of an
arbiter of States, came out with the motion, not
only in the words, but the very original paper that
was given him; and, with a confidence astonishing
to all, who were in the secret, he called it his own,
and said it was the result of his own reflections on
the subject, in the short intervals of ease, he had
enjoyed, during a most painful disorder. In this
pompous and farcical manner did he make that
famous proposition, upon which he and his adherents
have arrogated so much; but neither he nor they

have any other merit in the case, than an attempt to deceive both parties, can fairly entitle them. For, at the very time he was buoying up the hopes of the advocates, he was assuring the opposers of the Constitution, by his emissaries, that he was really averse to it; and upon the strictest scrutiny, we cannot find that any one vote was gained by his being ostensibly in favour of it. The votes of the Old Patriot, and Mr. Changeling, and Mr. Joyce, jun. we know were determined in its favour, by the resolutions of the mechanicks; but the votes of many others who used implicitly to follow Mr. H. were in the negative, which were counted upon by the friends of the Constitution, as being certain on their side. This is a strong confirmation that Mr. H. was then playing a game, which these people well understood; and indeed they, some of them, explicitly declared it at the time. His subsequent conduct, in regard to amendments, is a clear proof also, that by appearing in its favour in Convention, he did not mean to support it, and that he was not serious when he declared his proposition to be only conciliatory, and not to remedy any defects existing in his mind in the Constitution as reported, which he explicitly declared at the time was the case.

I feel a reluctance at exposing to the world this transaction, on various accounts; but when a man demands of us so much homage, and assumes to himself so much merit, for an action, which when rightly understood, must certainly render him very contemptible, I think the public should know how far they are indebted to him in the instance referred to. Has Mr. H. proved himself open and undisguised in this instance, as he assured the court in his message? Let him have the credit of it.—But if he has been guilty of repeated duplicity—if he has endeavoured to deceive both parties for his own private advantage, may he then meet the disapprobation he deserves.

—•—

NO. VIII.

WE have all a desire of appearing respectable in the eyes of the world; and have a strong relish for that kind of attention, which is generally shewn to eminent and worthy characters. This natural principle, when properly restrained, and under the guidance of reason, is highly useful. It stimulates to virtuous action; and gives us a taste for merited applause. But if it be permitted to operate too strongly on our minds, it will certainly injure our character in the end; and eventually deprive us of that small portion of fame which might otherwise have been readily allowed to us by the world. In proof of this, instances in life do very often occur; and among public men, we not unfrequently see, most humiliating proofs of the danger of indulging in inordinate love of popular applause. When in the course of events, a weak man is accidentally elevated, which in this country has sometimes happened, the parade of the office and the flattery of his venal dependents soon make him giddy ;—and if he has a native proneness to vanity, he will get to relish the grossest flattery, and will not only borrow, but take without leave the plumes of another to ornament himself. But of all the instances of indulging to a foolish vanity, and an undue passion for flattery and ostentation, those which Mr. H. has often exhibited, have been the most excessive ; and particularly the one which I mentioned in my last number, I mean his celebrated proposition in our State convention. Who that had not lost all sense of decency and modesty, could have so publickly declared, what many who heard him could not believe? Who that had not blunted his feelings, by gratefully receiving the most servile flattery, would have arrogated the merit of an action, or proposition, which many who heard him, knew to be the projection of another.

But that opportunity of increasing his borrowed reputation was too inviting to be omitted ; and the feather then offered him was of so enchanting a hue, that he could not resist the desire of wearing it; though he might have known, from the circumstances of the case, that it would soon fall from his crest. So entirely enslaved is he, by his vanity and caprice, that he in the instance referred to, for the purpose of extending his popularity and securing his post, appearedto be in favour of the Constitution in direct opposition to his own most deliberate resolutions, and against the most earnest remonstrances of the Old Patriot, Mr. Quondam, and Mr. Changeling. For though two of them voted for it, to please their constituents, it was generally known that they were secretly opposed to it, and privately assisted those members, who were openly against it. We cannot soon forget the old patriot's attempt to lose the question by an insidious motion by way of amendment; nor the celebrated speech of a conceited Eastern opposer, which was said to have been seen in the writing of Mr. Changeling. Nor can we believe, that the open opposition of Mr. Quondam would have been so conspicuous, or the secret attempts of the two others, to defeat the views of their patron, have been pursued, had his support to the question been more than ostensible; their uniform absolute devotedness to his will renders it incredible.

When the constitution was adopted by a number of the States, and there was a good prospect of its going through the Union, a new scene opened, to fire Mr. H.'s ambition. It was thought by the Cabinet, from the manner of electing the Presidents, that Mr. H. might, by a general vote in his favour, under the idea of his being second, possibly become the first president in the Union.—This was thought a very flattering idea to them all—for, if they could have succeeded, the whole junto would soon have been in office.—To promote these views a trusty hand was sent off to the Southern States, to solicit votes in his favour; and we soon saw the name of Mr. H. in all the papers from thence as the only one there thought of to be the second to Washington; and to compleat their folly, this same agent, as he himself said, before he sat off, attempted to draw from Dr. Adams, a relinquishment of any pretensions to the chair of Vice President, under the idea his being placed at the head of the Judiciary. But their views were too open to escape the Doctor's penetrating eye; and they and their proposition were treated with proper contempt.—Nor were they more successful in the other States—the name of Mr. H. appeared in their papers, during the time for which their agent had paid for its insertion; and it then disappeared, and has remained in obscurity, as to that object. In this instance, we cannot but wonder at the presumption and folly of that motly cabinet, in entertaining the idea, that Mr. H. could among men of sense, have any chance in competition with so great a character as Dr. Adams. The event has proved a great mortification to the vanity of Mr. H. and has shown most clearly the great disparity of their characters and merits in the minds of the electors through the Union. To compensate two of these principal adherents, the Patriot and the Changeling, for his appearance of opposition to

them with respect to the Constitution, Mr. H. assured them, that in his administration, he would
attend to their interest, and be guided by their ad-
vice.—This promise he has more religiously ob-
served, than any one he had ever before made.
He interfered in the elections to support the Patriot's pretensions—he insulted the man who was
the choice of the people—he violated the Constitution—he assumed a discretion to suspend the laws
—he treated repeatedly with very great indignity
his constitutional council, the most respectable that
I ever recollect; and he has wantonly vilified the
best men in the State, to promote the interest, and
gratify the feelings of two unworthy characters, the
Patriot and the Changeling. These things are of
so recent a date, and are so fresh in our minds,
that it cannot now be necessary to recite the facts.
We shall only observe, that he had become so vain
and confident, from the general support he received
at the last election, in consequence of the promise
he had from the advocates for the Constitution, as a reward for his apparently deserting his
friend in the State convention, that he has freely
indulged his whims and his feelings, and has
given full scope to his caprice and ill humour.—His
conduct has lately much more resembled the froward-
ness of a child, than the dignified elevation proper
to his station; and every branch of government has,
in its turn, experienced the inconvenience of his
puerile pettishness. The inconsistency and inde-

cency of his conduct, has been much more frequent
and conspicuous than ever, since he has been under
the management of the three characters we have
mentioned. Never was there in appearance, a more
extraordinary coalition.—Mr. H. has really no confidence in either of them; and he has repeatedly
declared, it is said, that he knows them all three to
be devoid of all principle.—How often have we
heard them all speak of each other, in the most
opprobrious manner; and openly declare, that they
were respectively governed by no other than the
most selfish motives? But Mr. H. and his advisers
have a common interest, which is opposite to that
of the publick. They all four are sensible, that
they depend only on the passions of the people for
their places and support. They know that a political calm, and a steady administration to Government, which would quiet the feelings of the people,
and leave them to the guidance of their sober reason, would soon deprive them of their political existence.—Hence we find, that nothing is so alarming
to them, as the appearance of publick tranquillity;
and upon the first symptoms of its approach, they
take their parts, and most industriously labour to
produce an irritation upon the publick mind.—They
have then immediate recourse to their threadbare
artifice, of exhibiting tories, jacobites and aristocrats
to arouse the people; and to give the farce an appearance of truth, they will fabricate and publish
letters about plots and treasons. The several members of this quadruple alliance have all been equally

conspicuous, allowing for the difference of the age
and opportunity, for their inordinate thirst for
places and preferment; and they have each of them,
in their turn, cursed the others most heartily, for
standing in their way, and have been equally emu-
lous in their imitations of Proteus.

Let any man review the political conduct of each
of the allies, with coolness and candour, free from
all prejudice against, or partiality in favour of them,
and he will have no doubt as to the principle of action. He will find, that ambition, or avarice has
uniformly directed them as public men, according
to the object before them; and that to attain their
points, they have with surprising facility, changed
their principles and their party, associating one day
and execrating the next, as their passions or their
interests have happened to dictate.

———◆———

NO. IX.

I HAVE been not a little diverted at the various
conjectures, as to the author of LACO; and have
been pleased to find, that after all their inquiries,
the friends of Mr. H. have been perfectly at a loss.
I am a plain, and a private man; and have no interest in the management of publick affairs, save only
as they may affect the people at large.—I live upon
a small patrimony, at a few miles' distance from
Boston, and have leisure to attend to measures and

men, as they pass before me; and being perfectly
independent of all parties, I care not who is in
or who is out of administration, so that Government
be well administered. All I want is, to have men
of virtue and integrity in office; and to guard
against the artifices of popular and selfish men, who
have too long had the reins of Government in their
hands. I can write as I please; and can be either
dull or poignant, as I think will best suit my purpose. No one can determine the writer from his
manner; for this he can and does vary at his pleasure. And the curious inquirers, I can assure you,
will never hit upon the true author, unless you should
by accident, come at the means of disclosing him.

I mean now, sir, to touch upon a few instances
of Mr. H.'s misconduct, which, as they were rather
aside from the common course of his official duty, I
did not notice in their order as to time. The sloop
Winthrop was at the earnest request of the people
in our eastern country, built by the Government to
protect their coast, from the depredations of the
British, and to guard their coasting vessels against
the small cruisers, which annoyed their trade. She
was manned and fitted by the State, for those purposes alone; and the Governour was desired as head
of the executive, to give the commander of her the
necessary orders, and to see that she was so employed,
as should best answer the purposes for which she
was equipped. And for a number of months she

was usefully improved, and afforded great relief, and protection to that far extended coast. But the captain of her finding that no rich prize was there to be met with; he earnestly and actually desired to extend the limits of his cruise. He applied to Mr. H. for permission to go among the West India Islands, and being backed by others, whom Mr. H. was willing to oblige, he, in opposition to the directions of the court, and the most earnest remonstrances of our merchants and eastern fellow-citizens, supported by their friends, gave him liberty to leave that country unguarded. The consequence was, that their trade was annihilated by the small refugee cruisers, and many very valuable prizes to our privateers, which took to that coast for a shelter, relying on the protection of the sloop, were again captured by the British.

When the British had determined, in consequence of an article in the treaty of peace, to deliver up Penobscot, they gave notice thereof to Congress, and desired that some person might be authorized to take possession of that post. That information was given by Congress to Mr. H. as Governour of this State, with a request that some proper person might be sent from hence to receive the post from the British. This gave Mr. H. a new opportunity, as he supposed, to make himself conspicuous, and he conceived the puerile, and absurd idea of going to Penobscot in person to

take the possession of it, without at all adverting
to the gross impropriety of the measure, arising
from the very great difference between his own
rank and that of the British officer who commanded
there. It is very extraordinary, and equally laugh-
able, that Mr. H. should at one time feel so highly
the dignity of his station, as to treat with contempt
a French Ambassador, the immediate representa-
tive of majesty; and at another be so very ready
to sacrifice his own honour, and the dignity of the
State of which he was the Governour, by descending
to a level with a major or a captain in the British
army. But he never did distinguish between
reality and appearance; and was always captivated with any thing that looked like parade. He
therefore had great preparations made for this
famous expedition, he hired a vessel to carry him
and his suite, which was to have consisted of a
multitude of aids, and all the military officers he
could prevail upon to attend him. After several
weeks' delay, he had formed his arrangements, and
he was ready for embarking; but an unfortunate
idea entered into his mind, and he conceived it was
possible, that the British might not be serious in
their proposal of delivering up the post, and that
he and his attendants might be there detained as pri-
soners. This damped his ardour for that famous expedition, and he began to think it were prudent to send
the Colonel of the Boston regiment of militia. Still,

however, he was very loth to give up the voyage; and between his vanity and his fears, a long time was suffered to pass away without any decision ; and he was at last relieved from the difficulty, by an account from Penobscot, that the commanding officer, conceiving himself very much neglected, having received no information from Mr. H. of what he was doing or intended, and tired of waiting for advices, had quitted the post, after burning the houses, and other public buildings, with the stores they contained. Thus did Mr. H. not only put the State to a very great expense in the hire of vessels, and making great preparations to gratify his pride and vanity ; but he lost also to the State, the valuable buildings which the British burnt from resentment. Had he sent off at once a proper officer, without any expense of money, or loss of time, what a saving of money, and reputation would have been made to the State. But this is one of the many instances, in which he has been wantonly lavish of both to gratify his vanity and caprice.

In a free government, the militia is justly considered as the natural and proper safeguard to the state. But in order to this, a military spirit must be cultivated, and a proper emulation to excel in the performance and knowledge of their duty must be excited, among both officers and soldiers. A conviction of this, and a sense of duty in the worthy predecessor of Mr. H., as Governour of the State, had led him to make a point of organizing and encouraging a proper emulation among the militia. Men of character, of spirit, and knowledge in military matters, were induced to take commissions; and, with the assistance of the generals, he had really got the militia of the State into very good order. The Boston regiment, in particular, made such an appearance in their manœuvres, when embodied, as did honour to the officers and the State, and they raised the admiration of every one who saw them. There certainly was nothing like them to be found in America; and foreigners very readily confessed that in their own countries there was nothing to equal them, of the kind. The importance of keeping up, and increasing the military ardour was very strongly impressed on every one's mind; for we had sorely experienced the want of a good militia during the late insurrections, and it was this, perhaps, in part, which had made the military spirit so very general and conspicuous. But no sooner did Mr. H. again fill the chair than that spirit of emulation began to subside. Both officers and men seemed universally to presage that, from the caprice of Mr. H., rank and promotion would no longer result from superior knowledge and abilities in the profession: but very justly expected that his adherents would very often, if not always, take the place of those who had a clear right, upon every principle, to promotion. This apprehension produced a visible effect upon the feelings and con-

duct of the militia; and we soon saw that their
expectations were well founded. He soon threw
the militia into confusion by his capricious conduct
in the appointment of officers, &c., and at length,
by the most wanton exercise of his prerogative, as
commander in chief, he wholly disbanded or broke
up the Boston regiment, the pride of the state. He
appointed a man to the office of adjutant general who
had no qualification for it but a pertness and assurance peculiar to himself, and who had no claim to
promotion of any kind but his being a relation to
Mr. H., and his having exerted himself, by most gross
misrepresentations in the publick papers, and probably by the privity of his patron, to prevent the
adoption of the Constitution by this State. By this
gross prostitution of the prerogative of office, and
by many other instances of selfishness and caprice,
Mr. H. has not only destroyed the most complete
regiment of militia ever known in America, but he
has damped the ardour of all the others, for they
find by experience that, while he is at the head,
merit and abilities will be frowned upon, and that
nothing but the grossest venality will give any one
a chance for promotion.

These are facts too notorious to be denied, or to
require a very minute statement of the proofs. Let
his puffers now come forward, and shew us in which
of these instances he discovered his patriotism and
regard for the welfare of society, or by which of

them he merits the arrogated title of "SAVIOUR OF HIS COUNTRY ;" or, rather let them satisfy us, if they can, that he has not in all of them sacrificed the interest of the public, by his ignorance of the duties of his office—by his selfishness, vanity and caprice, or what, perhaps, is worse, to promote his unworthy dependents.

———◆———

NO. X.

In a free, elective government like ours, the happiness, and even the safety of the community very much depends upon the prudence and discretion of the people, in their choice of persons, who are to administer it. In vain do we boast of our excellent constitution, if those who manage our publick affairs, are too weak or wicked to conform to its principles. A man may, in particular cases, be usefully elevated to important office on account merely of some exterior qualities, or adventitious circumstances; but having been accustomed to view him with respect, and taught to look up to him, for political purposes, as a man eminent for his superior good qualities, we at length get the habit so deeply rooted, that when the veil is withdrawn we are apt to distrust our own senses, and are with difficulty brought to believe and confess the illusion we have experienced. But unless we learn carefully to ex-

amine public characters, and to consider their conduct without partiality or prejudice, fear or favour,
we never shall form a right judgment of men for
publick life, nor have any tolerable assurance, that
our government will be well administered, or that
we be in any degree happier for having a good constitution. The view we have taken of the political
conduct of Mr. H. mostly clearly confirms the pre-
ceding observations; and furnishes a most striking
instance of the folly, and the danger to which we
may be exposed, by too great a reliance on exterior
appearances and too implicit a conformity to popular
opinion. We have thereby seen, that when a man has
been elevated, and for a long time supported in office, upon those principles, he may, by the inattention of the people and popular arts, which Mr. H.
and his adherents have so industriously made use of,
enjoy, without merit, the most important stations,
and become immoveable by those who first raised
him to importance.

I have now done for the present, with the inquiry
I proposed as to his publick character and conduct;
in doing which, I had no other object, than to call
the recollection and attention of the people to facts,
which are too notorious to be denied, and of which
it would be idle in me to go into the proofs, since
every man's mind, who has been a careful observer
of men and measures, must certainly be stored with
them: and I cannot see, upon a cool revision of what

I have written, a single fact that I think is mis-stated
or even coloured. If any one doubts as to any part
of the narrative, let him inquire of those, who from
their connection with Mr. H. as a public man at the
time, or who from being interested in the facts allu-
ded to, must have it in their power to give him sat-
isfaction; and not to go either to the personal friends,
the real dependants or warm advocates of Mr. H.,
nor to his zealous opponents, for candid information
—for from neither of these he can expect to get it.

I might have added a vast variety of less important misconduct: every one knows how people
have been detained, day after day, to get papers,
that wanted only his official signature to complete
them, but he was not to be disturbed in his pleasures, or he did not feel in the mood to use his pen.
We all have heard of his very whimsical conduct,
wh·n the Roxbury horse, &c., was to be reviewed—
he would and would not attend; and almost every
one recollects the various freaks, that marked his
conduct, as to the review at Braintree. The county
of Essex will not soon forget his pompous entrance
and passage through their towns; and the previous
pains, which were taken, by circulating letters, and
by active messengers, to notify his coming, and to
solicit attention. Nor will his council forget, that
he once summoned them to convene on a Thursday,
upon special and important business—that they
appeared at the time—notified him of their attend-

ance—but neither heard from, nor saw him, until next Tuesday, I think, though he was amusing himself, part of the time, with some convivial friends, at a certain storehouse, and he spent Monday at the review at Braintree. Nor ought the public to be ignorant of the many days' pay, which they have been at the expense of, without any benefit, by having his council, at other times, kept together without any business, waiting for his caprice to lead him to his duty. Instances of this kind of neglect and inattention to the interest of the publick, have been so very numerous and frequent, it would be needless to attempt a recital of them; but every man almost may recollect a sufficiency to satisfy himself, that private considerations and his personal feelings have governed his conduct. But to assist those, who have not attended to his political character and conduct, let us now take a very summary view of them from the facts we have stated, none of which have ever been attempted to be disproved.

Mr. H. was, as we have seen, at the early part of our contest with Britain, a young man with a very large fortune, and some exterior qualities well enough adapted to form a popular character; but with a disposition so very capricious, susceptible of flattery, and prone to vanity, it was very difficult to keep him steady and to render him, with all the advantages he possessed, beneficial to the public. These obstacles, however, did not discourage the once venerable old patriot, and his compeers in politicks, from persevering in their object of making him a useful agent in the cause; and they succeeded, after much labour and watching, so far as to fix him on their side, and to give him importance in the eyes of the people. But they were much disappointed, in the degree of advantage they derived from his being eventually with them. They could draw no aids from his fortune to relieve the pressing exigencies of the State; nor could they restrain his vanity, to make him act with consistency, decision or dignity : and, we have accordingly seen, that from his first entering into publick life, to his return from Congress, he always required a steady hand and a vigilant eye, to prevent him from running into the utmost excess of levity, or personal selfishness. We might reasonably have presumed, that the precepts and examples of the patriots who brought him forward and supported him in publick life would have had some effect upon Mr. H. and that his natural levity would have been checked, by several years' intercourse with such characters. But we find he had so long indulged his various passions, and had been so pampered by a tribe of sycophants, who were always around him, that he became extremely averse to every thing serious, and soon got to be a bitter enemy to those who attempted to arrest his attention, even for a moment to matters of importance. Conscious of his own want of merit, and persuaded that every thoughtful, steady man must soon grow weary of his being in the chair, and wish to displace him, he made an implicit obedience to his will, and devotedness to his interest the only conditions upon which he would appoint to office, and he used his prerogative as a weapon of defence, to encourage those who were enlisted in his service, and to annoy or intimidate those, who appeared to be startled or grieved at his excesses. Hence proceeded that swarm of unworthy officers, in the various branches of the Executive department, who disgraced the Government, and preyed upon the people, until they grew uneasy, and were ripe for rebellion. When the natural effects of his own foibles became visible, and he saw that his downfall was at hand, he endeavoured to save himself, and revive his popularity by the stale artifice of appearing desirous of returning to the state of a private citizen. This failed him, and he was deeply provoked and mortified to find himself reduced to a situation, in which he was deprived of the pageantry of State, and the glare of office, which used to veil his defects from the eyes of the multitude; and he soon set himself most industriously at work, to increase the popular irritation, which he had before excited by improper appointments. The distressing effects of the late insurrections, which we still feel, or recollect, ought to rouse our indignation against Mr. H. and his adherents, who, wantonly, or rather selfishly, involved us in that dreadful situation by misrepresentations, and solely for the purpose of again recovering the chair of Government. That this event was produced by their agency, cannot be doubted, when we recollect their conduct and language at that time—that he was supported universally by the insurgents at the next election—that papers with his name, and that of one of his principal agents were used as passports through the insurgents' lines, —and that even those who were devoted to justice, by the law of their country, were assured of and enjoyed his protection when again clothed with the prerogative of pardon.

Nor has he been more wise or prudent since he re-assumed the chair. He has exhibited to our view one uniform scene of neglect of duty, or prostitution of the powers of his office, from improper motives. He has wasted our money—retarded business—assumed a right of dispensing with the law—insulted his council—deprived the State of a good militia, its natural and only proper defence—refused appointments to good men, because of their virtues and qualities for office, and bestowed them on those who were wholly unfit, merely because they hailed him as their patron—he has treated some very respectable strangers with neglect; and to others he has descended in such a manner as to embarrass them, and disgrace his office; and to increase his own popularity, he has ostensibly advocated the most important question ever submitted to a people, while his emissaries were employed, night and day, in confirming its opposers; and yet this is the instance to which he has referred us to prove, that he is *open* and *undisguised* in his politicks.

But there is one point which Mr. H. and his adherents have yet in view, that is still more important than any they have hitherto aimed at—I mean —to lessen the influence, and to bring into disrepute the Supreme Court. That bench, from the respectability of their characters, the independence of their conduct, and the ability and integrity which mark their decisions, have long, and justly been considered, as the greatest security we have for our lives, liberty and property. The very same qualities and virtues, which render them so dear and important in the minds of the people at large, have made them the great object of the envy and hatred of Mr. H. and his adherents. Whilst they consider that bench as a check to their views, they cannot but wish to lessen their credit, and bring them into disrepute. And we accordingly find, that they seize every opportunity to speak of them disrespectfully, and have industriously sought for occasions to suggest, that this Court was too revered and were considered as of too much importance in the State. They have likened them to the famous Judge JEFFRIES, and their official conduct to that of the

Star Chamber in England; and they lose no opportunity to impress an idea, that the views and principles of that bench, are very dangerous and unfavourable to the liberties of the people. However extravagant and daring the attempt, it is nevertheless true, that Mr. H.'s cabinet counsellors have formed a deliberate system, to destroy the usefulness and respectability of that venerable bench; and every one who has any acquaintance with him, or his agents, may surely recollect sentiments, which they have repeatedly thrown out, plainly for the purpose of creating a prejudice against them;—particularly about the time and relative to the late insurrections. But I trust that the scales will soon fall from our eyes, which have so long obstructed our sight. We shall then be able to distinguish characters; and Mr. H. and his principal adherents will then be held in proper estimation; or rather they will then be viewed, not as the friends of the liberty and the happiness of the people, but as persons whose views and pursuits all centre in themselves.

LACO.

FINIS.

LaVergne, TN USA
15 February 2010
173134LV00001B/187/A